CÉSAR FRANCK SELECTED PIANO COMPOSITIONS

I0803969

GAIL SMITH

Online Audio

To access the online audio recording go to:
WWW.MELBAY.COM/31122MEB

MEL BAY®

WWW.MELBAY.COM

Contents

About the Author

Gail Smith

Gail Smith received her Bachelor of Fine Arts Degree from Florida Atlantic University. She did graduate studies at Westminster Choir College as well as research at the Mendelssohn Archives in Berlin.

Gail is one of the foremost arranger/composers and is the author of over 50 piano books published by Mel Bay Publications, Hal Leonard, FJH, Lorenz and has a hymn in the Trinity hymnal. Gail is the composer of a unique book of palindromes that contains pieces that sound the same played backwards or forward and has composed several "ambigrams" which sound the same upside down, ex. NOON.

Gail was the Music chairman for the Nations League of American Pen Women and president of the local chapter. She has taught students from the age of 3 to 99 and a 4-year-old blind student.

Gail has given workshops on improvisation and concerts all over the U.S. and in Sweden, Germany, and Japan. She has done extensive research on many women composers and is the author of *Four Centuries of Women Composers, The Music of Amy Beach, Women Composers in History*, and many others.

Gail gave a concert of Teresa Carreno's music at the Embassy of Venezuela and gave a concert in the historic Trinity Church in Boston where Amy Beach was married to celebrate Beach's 150th birthday. Portraying Clara Schumann in concerts brings every element of Gail's talent into focus.

Preface

The Life and Music of César Franck
(Born 1822 – Died 1890)

César Auguste Franck was born in Liege, Belgium on December10, 1822. From the time he was born his father was determined to have him become a concert pianist. When César was very young he was enrolled in the conservatory in their home town and began piano lessons.

At the age of twelve César had completed his studies there and in 1835 the family moved to Paris. César was enrolled in the Paris Conservatory and began studies in Counterpoint and Fugue. He began composing and won the First Prize in Fugue in 1838. César performed the "Concerto in A minor" by Hummel, which was the required test piece. During the sight-reading test, César decided to transpose the piece a third down but Cherbini, who was the judge, refused to award the first prize to the "irreverent" contestant. The jury however decided to give an award designated: "Grand Priz d' honneur" to César Franck. It was the only time such an award was given at the Paris Conservatory.

While still a student at the Conservatory, César composed three trios that his father directed him to dedicate to H.M. Leopold I, King of Belgium. In April of 1842, César's father abruptly forced him to leave the Conservatory and take up the career of a "virtuoso".

For the next few years, César gave concerts and taught piano lessons while living at home. These concerts provided his father's source of income. César composed most of his piano works during this time.

France had a paternal authority law that required a son to have his father's permission to marry if he wasn't the legal age of 25. César had been in love for a long time to a young lady at the conservatory. This caused a turbulent time with his father that persisted until he turned 25 years of age. He finally got married in 1848 and César began a new chapter of his life.

César gave up his concert career and became organist of St. Clothilde. He also taught ten hours a day at the conservatory. Cesar usually spent the first two hours of each day composing. César composed the famous "Symphony in D minor", two operas, the violin sonata, string quartets, and numerous choral works.

César Franck died on November 8, 1890. His pupils included Faure, d'Indy, and many others who called him "a teaching saint."

The pieces in this book will give you a sampling of the beautiful, interesting piano works that César Franck composed for his performances and his students. His friends said that when he found a new chord, it made him happy all day. An example of this can be found in "Danse Lente". Compare measure 25 with measure 37. When you play this, you can hear the subtle change that one note can make.

I'm sure as you practice these pieces it will give you a glimpse into the skill this composer used to create interesting melodies and develop patterns.

Earliest Composition

César Franck

Canon

César Franck

Poco animato

poco cresc.
ben legato
dolcissimo

Andantino in E Minor

César Franck

Andantino

Les Plaintes d'Une Poupée

César Franck

Andantino

20
dolcissimo
25
poco rall.
p molto legato
30
cresc.
dim.
p
35
p
cresc.

40
dim.
p
45
dolce
51
poco piú
f
57
dim. e rall.

Andante in D Major

César Franck

Quasi andante

17
p
20
cresc.
poco rit.
a tempo
23
pp
rall.
26

Lento in C Minor

César Franck

Poco lento

14
cresc.
17
dim.
p
20
23
dim.
pp

Minuet in A Flat

Allegretto amabile

César Franck

19
p poco cresc.
23
dim.
pp
27
molto cresc.
f
p
31
36
rall.
pp

Andantino in A Major

8

César Franck

Andantino

poco accel.
rall.
13
f
p
a tempo
16
p
20
sempre dolce
(mp)
23
(p)

Danse Lente

Quasi lento (𝅗𝅥 = 63)

César Franck

21
poco piú f
25
f
dim.
p
29
cantabile
rall.
pp
33
a tempo
piú f
cresc.
37
f
dim.
p
41
Poco piú lento
tristamente
rall.
p
8va
pp

10

Andantino in A Flat

César Franck

13
mf
16
19
22
f

25
28
poco dim.
p cresc.
31
mf
f
34
rall.
dim.
p